Quilts
TO CROCHET

Get ready to impress your friends with eye-catching crocheted "quilts." Five stunning afghans reflecting popular quilt patterns are created using only the half double crochet stitch, but a unique way to change colors makes these throws challenging and rewarding. Designer Barbara Faul's technique for color changes ensures a smooth transition, giving her afghans a polished look. Detailed instructions explain the easiest way to complete these color changes, using bobbins or even "jaw" hair clips to keep colors separated. Practice swatch instructions and diagrams are included for intermediate designs, and gorgeous photographs show you exactly what the finished quilts will look like. So take the time to create one of these striking afghans — they're worth it!

GENERAL INSTRUCTIONS

ABBREVIATIONS

ch(s)	chain(s)
cm	centimeters
hdc	half double crochet(s)
mm	millimeters
Rnd(s)	Round(s)
sp(s)	space(s)
YO	yarn over

★ — work instructions following ★ as many **more** times as indicated in addition to the first time.

† to † — work all instructions from first † to second † **as many** times as specified.

( ) — work enclosed instructions **as many** times as specified by the number immediately following **or** work all enclosed instructions in the stitch or space indicated **or** contains explanatory remarks.

colon (:) — the number(s) given after a colon at the end of a row or round denote(s) the number of stitches or spaces you should have on that row or round.

GAUGE

Exact gauge is essential for proper size. Before beginning your Afghan, make the sample swatch given in the individual instructions in the yarn and hook specified. After completing the swatch, measure it, counting your stitches and rows carefully. If your swatch is larger or smaller than specified, make another, changing hook size to get the correct gauge. Keep trying until you find the size hook that will give you the specified gauge.

BOBBINS

Bobbins are used to hold the small amount of yarn needed to work each color change and also to help keep the different colored yarns from tangling. Start each bobbin as you would a new ball of yarn, leaving a 6" end to weave in later. Only unfasten enough yarn to work the area comfortably, otherwise they will tangle.

Options for Bobbins: Knitting bobbins, bobby pins, or small jaw hair clips.

◖☐☐☐ **BEGINNER**	Projects for first-time crocheters using basic stitches. Minimal shaping.
◖◼☐☐ **EASY**	Projects using yarn with basic stitches, repetitive stitch patterns, simple color changes, and simple shaping and finishing.
◖◼◼☐ **INTERMEDIATE**	Projects using a variety of techniques, such as basic lace patterns or color patterns, mid-level shaping and finishing.
◖◼◼◼ **EXPERIENCED**	Projects with intricate stitch patterns, techniques and dimension, such as non-repeating patterns, multi-color techniques, fine threads, small hooks, detailed shaping and refined finishing.

CROCHET TERMINOLOGY	
UNITED STATES	**INTERNATIONAL**
slip stitch (slip st) =	single crochet (sc)
single crochet (sc) =	double crochet (dc)
half double crochet (hdc) =	half treble crochet (htr)
double crochet (dc) =	treble crochet (tr)
treble crochet (tr) =	double treble crochet (dtr)
double treble crochet (dtr) =	triple treble crochet (ttr)
skip =	miss

Yarn Weight Symbol & Names	SUPER FINE 1	FINE 2	LIGHT 3	MEDIUM 4	BULKY 5	SUPER BULKY 6
Type of Yarns in Category	Sock, Fingering, Baby	Sport, Baby	DK, Light Worsted	Worsted, Afghan, Aran	Chunky, Craft, Rug	Bulky, Roving

ALUMINUM CROCHET HOOKS												
U.S.	B-1	C-2	D-3	E-4	F-5	G-6	H-8	I-9	J-10	K-10½	N	P	Q
Metric - mm	2.25	2.75	3.25	3.5	3.75	4	5	5.5	6	6.5	9	10	15

JOINING WITH HDC

When instructed to join with hdc, begin with a slip knot on hook. YO, holding loop on hook, insert hook in space indicated, YO and pull up a loop, YO and draw through all 3 loops on hook.

CHANGING COLORS

The basic color change is always worked the same. For the color changes to look smooth, on the row after the color change, you need to work over the strand that was created when changing colors. Make a swatch to practice changing colors in the desired color pattern.

BASIC COLOR CHANGE AND AT END OF ROW

YO, insert hook in st or sp indicated, YO and pull up a loop, drop yarn, with new color *(Fig. 1)*, YO and draw through all 3 loops on hook.

Fig. 1

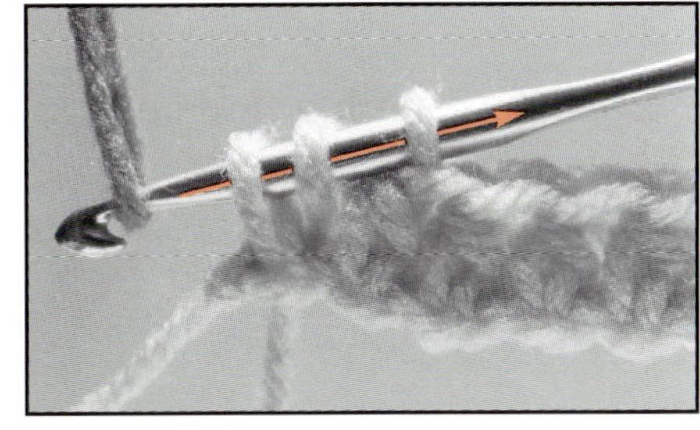

Work basic color change dropping yarn to **front** of work.
When working the **next** row, insert hook under strand of same color as space you are working into **and** in space *(Figs. 2a & b)*.

Fig. 2a

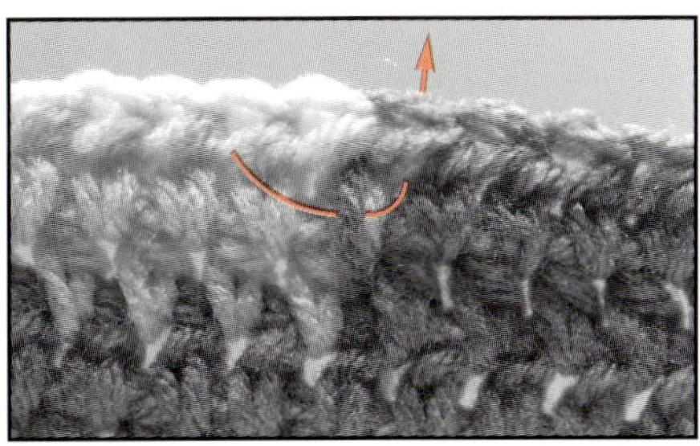

Fig. 2b

If the yarn will be carried one stitch on the same row as the color change, insert hook in space **and** under the next color *(Fig. 3)*.

Fig. 3

WORKING IN SPACE BEFORE AN HDC

When instructed to work in space **before** an hdc, insert hook in space indicated by arrow *(Fig. 4)*.

Fig. 4

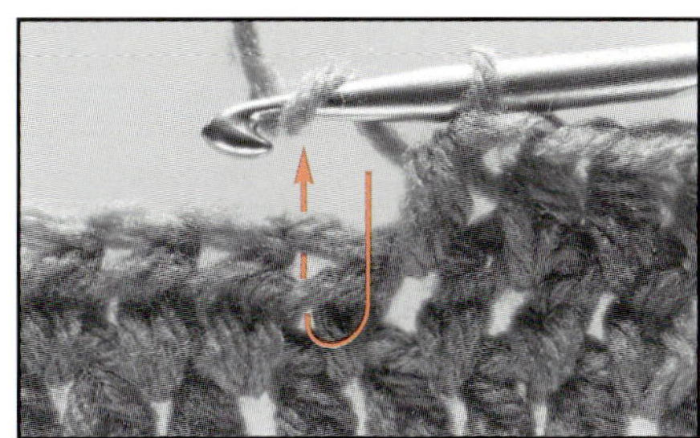

1. LOG CABIN

■■□□ EASY

Finished Size: 63¹/₂" (161.5 cm) square

MATERIALS

Worsted Weight Yarn: **MEDIUM 4**
Lt Blue - 21 ounces, 1,260 yards
(600 grams, 1,152 meters)
Green, Variegated, Blue, **and** Purple -
12¹/₂ ounces, 750 yards
(360 grams, 686 meters) **each**
Crochet hook, size H (5 mm) **or** size needed
for gauge

GAUGE: In pattern, 11 hdc = 4" (10 cm);
12 rows = 4¹/₄" (10.75 cm)

Work hdc in space **before** next hdc *(Fig. 4, page 3)* and in space **before** turning ch throughout.

Gauge Swatch: 4"w x 4¹/₄"h
(10 cm x 10.75 cm)
With Lt Blue, ch 12.
Row 1: Hdc in second ch from hook and in each ch across: 11 hdc.
Rows 2-12: Ch 1, turn; hdc in first sp and in each sp across.
Finish off.

AFGHAN
CENTER
With Lt Blue, ch 11.

Row 1: Hdc in second ch from hook and in each ch across: 10 hdc.

Work hdc in space **before** next hdc *(Fig. 4, page 3)* and in space **before** turning ch throughout.

Row 2 (Right side)**:** Ch 1, turn; hdc in first sp and in each sp across.

Note: Loop a short piece of yarn around any stitch to mark Row 2 as **right** side.

Rows 3-10: Ch 1, turn; hdc in first sp and in each sp across; at end of Row 10, change to Green in last hdc made *(Fig. 1, page 3)*; cut Lt Blue.

SECTION 1

Row 1: Ch 1, do **not** turn; hdc in end of each row across Center: 10 hdc.

Rows 2-4: Ch 1, turn; hdc in first sp and in each sp across.

Row 5: Ch 1, turn; hdc in first sp and in each sp across changing to Variegated in last hdc made; cut Green.

SECTION 2

Row 1: Ch 1, do **not** turn; hdc in end of each row across Section 1; working over beginning ch and in sps **before** hdc, hdc in first sp and in each sp across: 15 hdc.

Rows 2-4: Ch 1, turn; hdc in first sp and in each sp across.

Row 5: Ch 1, turn; hdc in first sp and in each sp across changing to Blue in last hdc made; cut Variegated.

SECTION 3

Row 1: Ch 1, do **not** turn; hdc in end of each row across Section 2 and across Center: 15 hdc.

Rows 2-4: Ch 1, turn; hdc in first sp and in each sp across.

Row 5: Ch 1, turn; hdc in first sp and in each sp across changing to Purple in last hdc made; cut Blue.

Continued on page 6

1
5

SECTION 4

Row 1: Ch 1, do **not** turn; hdc in end of each row across Section 3; working in sps across Row 10 of Center, hdc in first sp and in each sp across; hdc in end of each row across Section 1: 20 hdc.

Rows 2-4: Ch 1, turn; hdc in first sp and in each sp across.

Row 5: Ch 1, turn; hdc in first sp and in each sp across changing to Lt Blue in last hdc made; cut Purple.

SECTION 5

Row 1: Ch 1, do **not** turn; hdc in end of each row across last Section; working in sps across Row 5 of next Section, hdc in first sp and in each sp across; hdc in end of each row across next Section.

Rows 2-4: Ch 1, turn; hdc in first sp and in each sp across.

Row 5: Ch 1, turn; hdc in first sp and in each sp across changing to Green; cut previous color.

SECTION 6

Row 1: Ch 1, do **not** turn; hdc in end of each row across last Section; working in sps across Row 5 of next Section, hdc in first sp and in each sp across; hdc in end of each row across next Section.

Rows 2-4: Ch 1, turn; hdc in first sp and in each sp across.

Row 5: Ch 1, turn; hdc in first sp and in each sp across changing to Variegated; cut previous color.

SECTION 7

Row 1: Ch 1, do **not** turn; hdc in end of each row across last Section; working in sps across Row 5 of next Section, hdc in first sp and in each sp across; hdc in end of each row across next Section.

Rows 2-4: Ch 1, turn; hdc in first sp and in each sp across.

Row 5: Ch 1, turn; hdc in first sp and in each sp across changing to Blue; cut previous color.

SECTION 8

Row 1: Ch 1, do **not** turn; hdc in end of each row across last Section; working in sps across Row 5 of next Section, hdc in first sp and in each sp across; hdc in end of each row across next Section.

Rows 2-4: Ch 1, turn; hdc in first sp and in each sp across.

Row 5: Ch 1, turn; hdc in first sp and in each sp across changing to Purple; cut previous color.

SECTION 9

Row 1: Ch 1, do **not** turn; hdc in end of each row across last Section; working in sps across Row 5 of next Section, hdc in first sp and in each sp across; hdc in end of each row across next Section.

Rows 2-4: Ch 1, turn; hdc in first sp and in each sp across.

Row 5: Ch 1, turn; hdc in first sp and in each sp across changing to Lt Blue; cut previous color.

SECTIONS 10-64

Repeat Sections 5-9, 11 times.

SECTION 65

Row 1: Ch 1, do **not** turn; hdc in end of each row across last Section; working in sps across Row 5 of next Section, hdc in first sp and in each sp across; hdc in end of each row across next Section.

Rows 2-4: Ch 1, turn; hdc in first sp and in each sp across.

Row 5: Ch 1, turn; hdc in first sp and in each sp across; do **not** change colors and do **not** cut Lt Blue.

SECTIONS 66-68

Row 1: Ch 1, do **not** turn; hdc in end of each row across last Section; working in sps across Row 5 of next Section, hdc in first sp and in each sp across; hdc in end of each row across next Section.

Rows 2-5: Ch 1, turn; hdc in first sp and in each sp across.

At end of Section 68, finish off.

2. DOUBLE IRISH CHAIN

Shown on page 10.

■■■□ INTERMEDIATE

Finished Size: 56" x 69" (142 cm x 175.5 cm)

MATERIALS

Worsted Weight Yarn: MEDIUM 4

Brown - 32 ounces, 1,760 yards
(910 grams, 1,609.5 meters)
Tan - 29¹/₂ ounces, 1,625 yards
(840 grams, 1,486 meters)
Black - 13¹/₂ ounces, 745 yards
(380 grams, 681 meters)
Crochet hook, size H (5 mm) **or** size needed
for gauge
Bobbins or jaw hair clips

GAUGE: In pattern, 11 hdc = 4" (10 cm);
12 rows = 4¹/₄" (10.75 cm)

Work hdc in space **before** next hdc *(Fig. 4, page 3)* and in space **before** turning ch throughout.

Gauge Swatch: 4"w x 4¹/₄"h
(10 cm x 10.75 cm)
With Tan, ch 12.
Row 1: Hdc in second ch from hook and in each ch across: 11 hdc.
Rows 2-12: Ch 1, turn; hdc in first sp and in each sp across.
Finish off.

Wind each color onto bobbins *(see Bobbins, page 2)*. It is strongly recommended that you work the outlined square of the chart, page 9, as a process of familiarizing yourself with the color changes *(see Changing Colors, page 3)* and working with bobbins. This will also aid you in determining the yardage needed for each bobbin in the design.

AFGHAN BODY

With Brown, ch 146.

Row 1 (Right side)**:** Hdc in second ch from hook and in next 4 chs changing to Black in last hdc made, ★ † hdc in next 5 chs changing to Brown in last hdc made, hdc in next 5 chs changing to Tan in last hdc made, hdc in next 15 chs changing to Brown in last hdc made, hdc in next 5 chs changing to Black in last hdc made, hdc in next 5 chs changing to Brown in last hdc made †, hdc in next 5 chs changing to Tan in last hdc made, hdc in next 5 chs changing to Brown in last hdc made, hdc in next 5 chs changing to Black in last hdc made; repeat from ★ once **more**, then repeat from † to † once, hdc in last 5 chs: 145 hdc.

Note: Loop a short piece of yarn around any stitch to mark Row 1 as **right** side.

Work hdc in space **before** next hdc *(Fig. 4, page 3)* and in space **before** turning ch throughout.

Continue changing colors in same manner throughout.

Rows 2-4: Ch 1, turn; hdc in first sp and in next 4 sps changing to Black, ★ † hdc in next 5 sps changing to Brown, hdc in next 5 sps changing to Tan, hdc in next 15 sps changing to Brown, hdc in next 5 sps changing to Black, hdc in next 5 sps changing to Brown †, hdc in next 5 sps changing to Tan, hdc in next 5 sps changing to Brown, hdc in next 5 sps changing to Black; repeat from ★ once **more**, then repeat from † to † once, hdc in last 5 sps.

Continued on page 8.

Row 5: Ch 1, turn; hdc in first 5 sps changing to Black, ★ † hdc in next 5 sps changing to Brown, hdc in next 5 sps changing to Tan, hdc in next 15 sps changing to Brown, hdc in next 5 sps changing to Black, hdc in next 5 sps changing to Brown, hdc in next 5 sps changing to Tan †, hdc in next 5 sps changing to Brown, hdc in next 5 sps changing to Black; repeat from ★ once **more**, then repeat from † to † once.

Rows 6-51: Follow Chart below.

Rows 52-185: Follow Chart Rows 2-51 twice, then Rows 2-35 once **more**; at end of Row 185, do **not** change colors; cut Tan and Black.

COLOR KEY

▲ brown	★ black	☐ tan

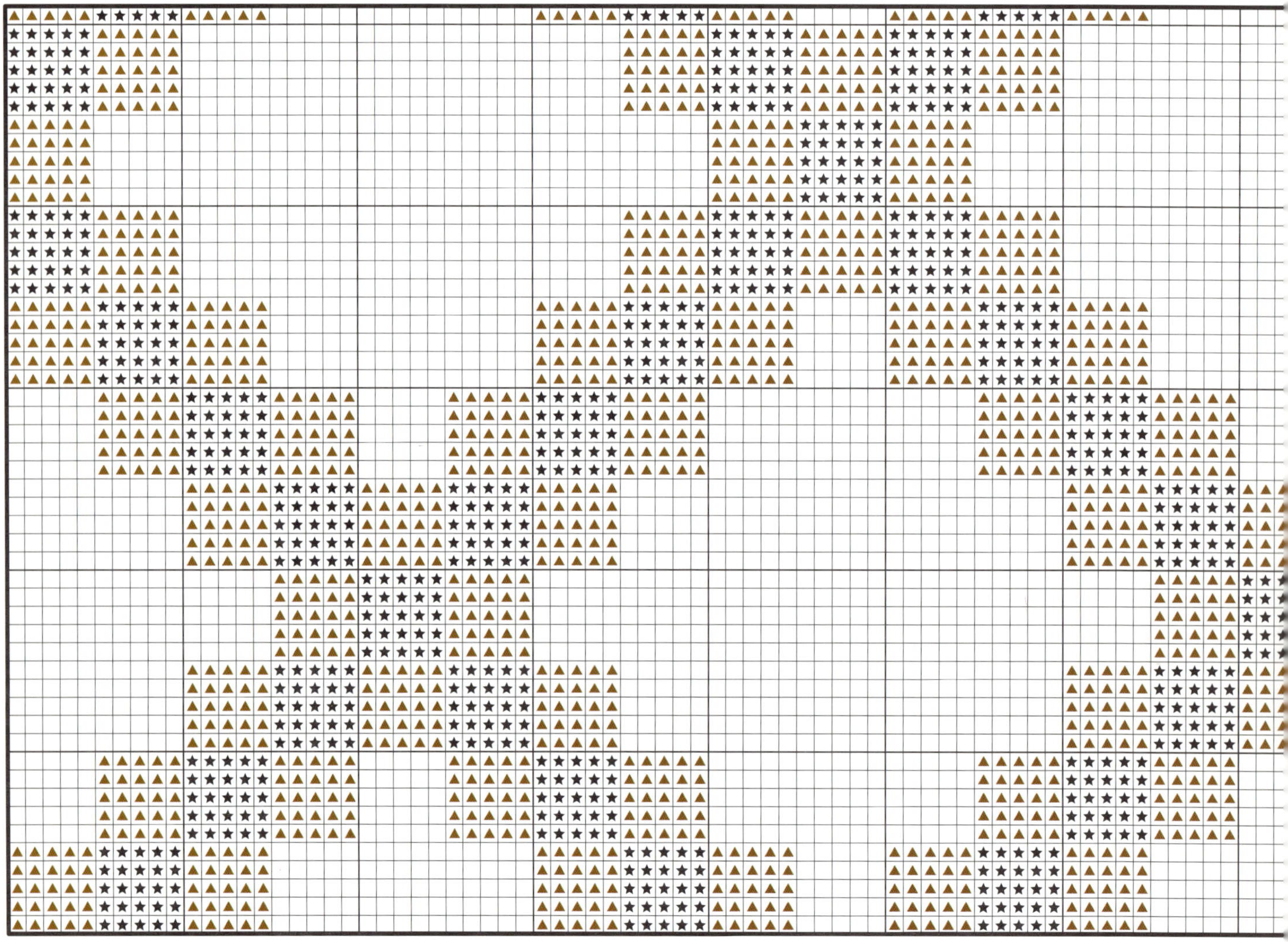

EDGING

Rnd 1: Ch 1, do **not** turn; 3 hdc in sp **before** last hdc made; working in end of rows, skip first row, hdc in next row and in each row across to last row, skip last row; working over beginning ch and in sps **before** hdc, 3 hdc in first sp and in each sp across to last sp, 3 hdc in last sp; working in end of rows, skip first row, hdc in next row and in each row across to last row, skip last row; working in sps across Row 185, 3 hdc in first sp, hdc in next sp and in each sp across; join with slip st to first hdc: 564 hdc.

Rnd 2: (Slip st, ch 1, hdc) in first sp, 2 hdc in next sp, ★ hdc in next sp and in each sp across to next corner 3-hdc group, 2 hdc in each of next 2 sps; repeat from ★ 2 times **more**, hdc in next sp and in each sp across, hdc in same sp as first hdc; join with slip st to first hdc.

Rnd 3: (Slip st, ch 1, 3 hdc) in first sp, ★ hdc in next sp and in each sp across to second hdc of first 2-hdc group, 3 hdc in next sp; repeat from ★ 2 times **more**, hdc in next sp and in each sp across; join with slip st to first hdc.

Rnds 4 and 5: Repeat Rnds 2 and 3.

Finish off.

On **right** side rows, work Chart from **right** to **left**; on **wrong** side rows, work Chart from **left** to **right**.

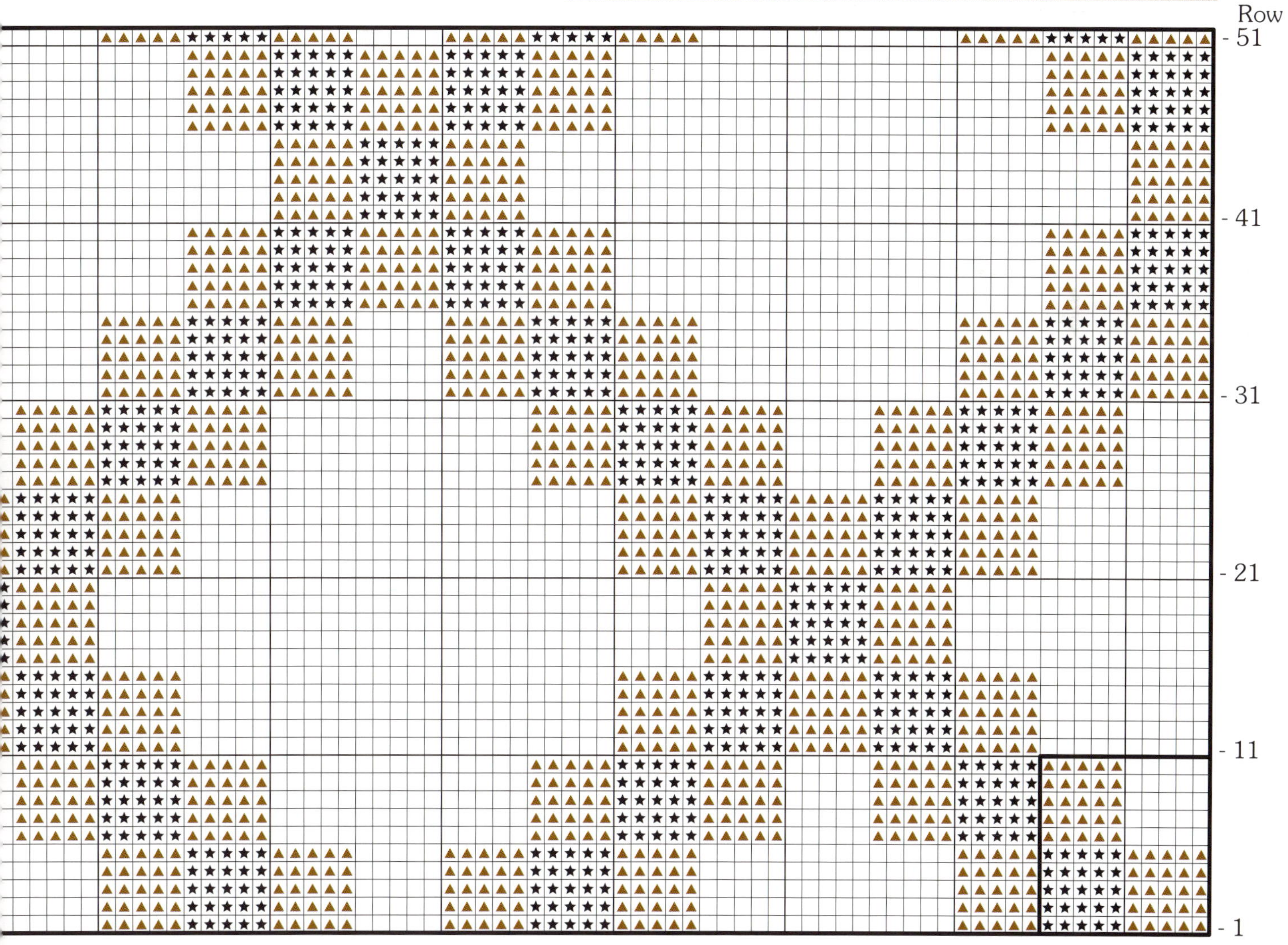

2

5

3. PINWHEEL
Shown on Front Cover.

INTERMEDIATE

Finished Size: 59" x 67" (150 cm x 170 cm)

MATERIALS

Worsted Weight Yarn: **MEDIUM 4**
   Lt Coral, Lt Green, **and** Green -
     14 ounces, 840 yards
       (400 grams, 768 meters) **each**
   Yellow **and** Coral - 13^1/$_2$ ounces, 810 yards
     (380 grams, 740.5 meters) **each**
Crochet hook, size H (5 mm) **or** size needed
   for gauge
Bobbins or jaw hair clips

GAUGE: In pattern, 11 hdc = 4" (10 cm);
       12 rows = 4^1/$_4$" (10.75 cm)

Work hdc in space **before** next hdc *(Fig. 4, page 3)* and in space **before** turning ch throughout.

Gauge Swatch: 4"w x 4^1/$_4$"h
         (10 cm x 10.75 cm)
With Yellow, ch 12.
Row 1: Hdc in second ch from hook and in each ch across: 11 hdc.
Rows 2-12: Ch 1, turn; hdc in first sp and in each sp across.
Finish off.

Wind each color onto bobbins *(see Bobbins, page 2)*. It is strongly recommended that you work the outlined square of the chart, page 13, as a process of familiarizing yourself with the color changes *(see Changing Colors, page 3)* and working with bobbins. This will also aid you in determining the yardage needed for each bobbin in the design.

Continued on page 14.

COLOR KEY

yellow   lt coral   coral   lt green   green

AFGHAN BODY

With Yellow, ch 153.

Row 1 (Right side)**:** Hdc in second ch from hook and in next 18 chs changing to Green in last hdc made, hdc in next 19 chs changing to Lt Green in last hdc made, hdc in next 19 chs changing to Lt Coral in last hdc made, hdc in next 19 chs changing to Coral in last hdc made, hdc in next 19 chs changing to Yellow in last hdc made, hdc in next 19 chs changing to Green in last hdc made, hdc in next 19 chs changing to Lt Green in last hdc made, hdc in last 19 chs changing to Lt Coral in last hdc: 152 hdc.

Note: Loop a short piece of yarn around any stitch to mark Row 1 as **right** side.

Work hdc in space **before** next hdc *(Fig. 4, page 3)* and in space **before** turning ch throughout.

Continue changing colors in same manner throughout.

Row 2: Ch 1, turn; hdc in first sp changing to Lt Green, † hdc in next 17 sps changing to Green, hdc in next sp changing to Lt Green, hdc in next sp changing to Green, hdc in next 17 sps changing to Yellow, hdc in next sp changing to Green, hdc in next sp changing to Yellow, hdc in next 17 sps changing to Coral †, hdc in next sp changing to Yellow, hdc in next sp changing to Coral, hdc in next 17 sps changing to Lt Coral, hdc in next sp changing to Coral, hdc in next sp changing to Lt Coral, hdc in next 17 sps changing to Lt Green, hdc in next sp changing to Lt Coral, hdc in next sp changing to Lt Green, repeat from † to † once, hdc in last sp.

Rows 3-180: Follow Chart, pages 12 and 13, Rows 3-101, then Rows 2-80 once **more**; at end of Row 180, finish off Green and cut all remaining colors.

EDGING

Rnd 1: With **right** side facing and working in sps across Row 180, join Yellow with hdc in first sp *(see Joining With Hdc, page 2)*; 2 hdc in same sp, hdc in next sp and in each sp across to last sp, 3 hdc in last sp; working in end of rows, skip first row, hdc in next row and in each row across to last row, skip last row; working over beginning ch and in sps **before** hdc, 3 hdc in first sp, hdc in next sp and in each sp across to last sp, 3 hdc in last sp; working in end of rows, skip first row, hdc in next row and in each row across to last row, skip last row; join with slip st to first hdc, finish off: 668 hdc.

Rnd 2: With **right** side facing, join Green with hdc in first sp **after** joining; 2 hdc in next sp, ★ hdc in next sp and in each sp across to next corner 3-hdc group, 2 hdc in each of next 2 sps; repeat from ★ 2 times **more**, hdc in next sp and in each sp across, hdc in same sp as first hdc; join with slip st to first hdc, finish off.

Rnd 3: With **right** side facing, join Lt Green with hdc in first sp **after** joining; 2 hdc in same sp, ★ hdc in next sp and in each sp across to second hdc of first 2-hdc group, 3 hdc in next sp; repeat from ★ 2 times **more**; hdc in next sp and in each sp across; join with slip st to first hdc, finish off.

Rnd 4: With Lt Coral, repeat Rnd 2.

Rnd 5: With Coral, repeat Rnd 3.

4. WHIRLIGIG

Shown on page Back Cover.

▰▰▰▱ INTERMEDIATE

Finished Size: 62" x 74¹/₂" (157.5 cm x 189 cm)

MATERIALS

Worsted Weight Yarn: **MEDIUM 4**
  Yellow **and** Blue - 37¹/₂ ounces, 2,250 yards
    (1,070 grams, 2,057.5 meters) **each**
Crochet hook, size H (5 mm) **or** size needed
  for gauge
Bobbins or jaw hair clips

GAUGE: In pattern, 11 hdc = 4" (10 cm);
       12 rows = 4¹/₄" (10.75 cm)

Work hdc in space **before** next hdc *(Fig. 4, page 3)* and in space **before** turning ch throughout.

Gauge Swatch: 4"w x 4¹/₄"h
              (10 cm x 10.75 cm)
With Yellow, ch 12.
Row 1: Hdc in second ch from hook and in each ch across: 11 hdc.
Rows 2-12: Ch 1, turn; hdc in first sp and in each sp across.
Finish off.

Wind each color onto bobbins *(see Bobbins, page 2)*. It is strongly recommended that you work the outlined square of the chart, page 17, as a process of familiarizing yourself with the color changes *(see Changing Colors, page 3)* and working with bobbins. This will also aid you in determining the yardage needed for each bobbin in the design.

AFGHAN BODY

With Blue, ch 161.

Row 1 (Right side)**:** Hdc in second ch from hook and in next 9 chs changing to Yellow in last hdc made, † hdc in next 10 chs changing to Blue in last hdc made, hdc in next 20 chs changing to Yellow in last hdc made, hdc in next 10 chs changing to Blue in last hdc made, hdc in next 9 chs changing to Yellow in last hdc made †, hdc in next 21 chs changing to Blue in last sc made, hdc in next 10 chs changing to Yellow in last hdc made, repeat from † to † once, hdc in last 21 chs: 160 hdc.

Note: Loop a short piece of yarn around any stitch to mark Row 1 as **right** side.

Work hdc in space **before** next hdc *(Fig. 4, page 3)* and in space **before** turning ch throughout.

Continue changing colors in same manner throughout.

Row 2: Ch 1, turn; hdc in first sp and in next 8 sps changing to Blue, † hdc in next 2 sps changing to Yellow, hdc in next 11 sps changing to Blue, hdc in next 9 sps changing to Yellow, hdc in next 9 sps changing to Blue, hdc in next 9 sps changing to Yellow, hdc in next 2 sps changing to Blue, hdc in next 10 sps changing to Yellow, hdc in next 10 sps changing to Blue †, hdc in next 9 sps changing to Yellow, hdc in next 9 sps changing to Blue, repeat from † to † once, hdc in last 9 sps.

Continued on page 16.

Rows 3-80: Follow Chart below.

Rows 81-200: Follow Chart Rows 1-80, then Rows 1-40 once **more**; at end of Row 200, do **not** finish off; cut Yellow.

COLOR KEY

☐ yellow	☒ blue

EDGING

Rnd 1: Ch 1, turn; 3 hdc in first sp, hdc in next sp and in each sp across to last sp, 3 hdc in last sp; working in end of rows, skip first row, hdc in next row and in each row across to last row, skip last row; working over beginning ch and in sps **before** hdc, 3 hdc in first sp, hdc in next sp and in each sp across to last sp, 3 hdc in last sp; working in end of rows, skip first row, hdc in next row and in each row across to last row, skip last row; join with slip st to first hdc: 724 hdc.

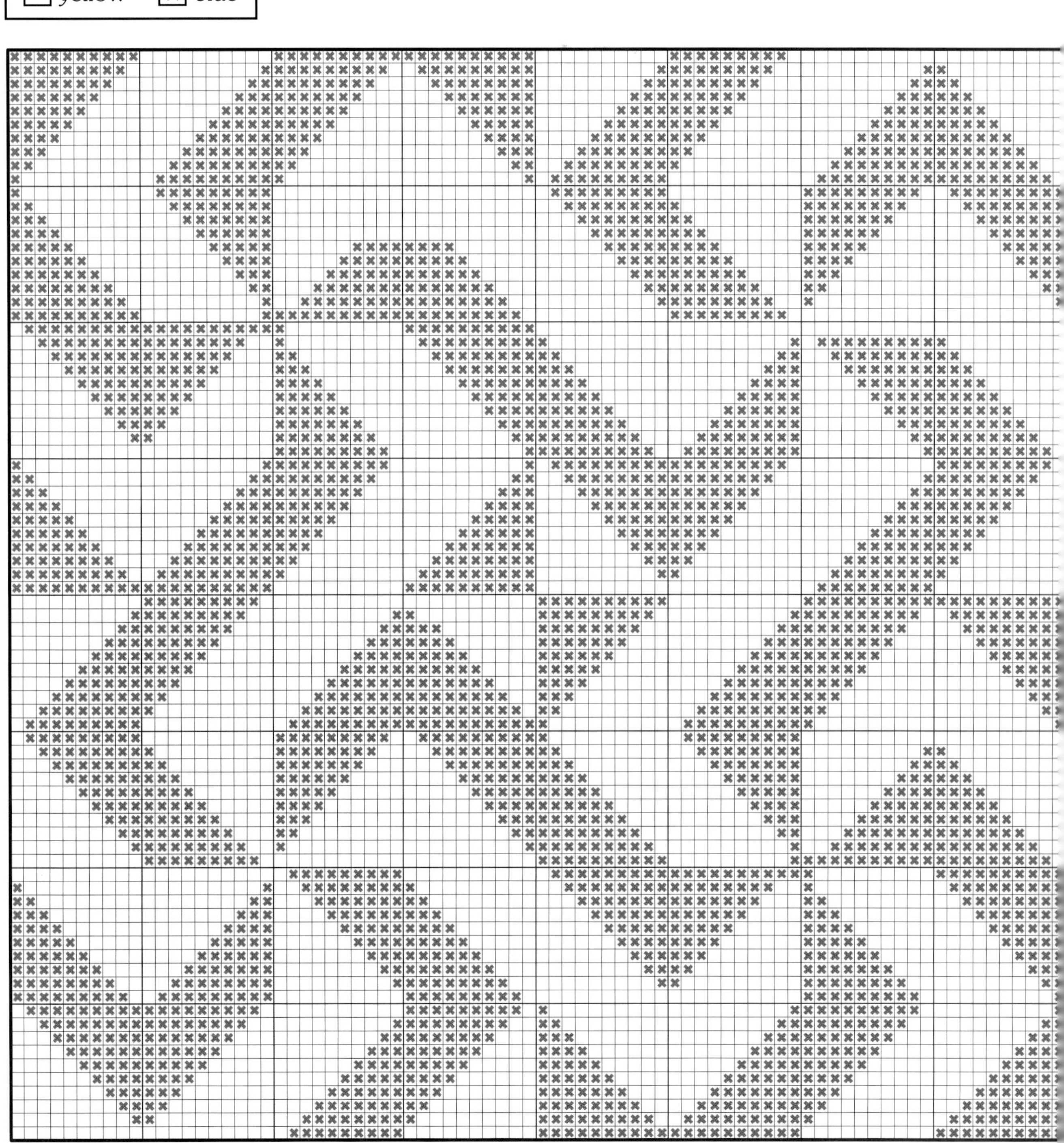

Rnd 2: (Slip st, ch 1, hdc) in first sp, 2 hdc in next sp, ★ hdc in next sp and in each sp across to next corner 3-hdc group, 2 hdc in each of next 2 sps; repeat from ★ 2 times **more**, hdc in next sp and in each sp across, hdc in same sp as first hdc; join with slip st to first hdc.

Rnd 3: (Slip st, ch 1, 3 hdc) in first sp, ★ hdc in next sp and in each sp across to second hdc of first 2-hdc group, 3 hdc in next sp; repeat from ★ 2 times **more**; hdc in next sp and in each sp across; join with slip st to first hdc.

Rnds 4 and 5: Repeat Rnds 2 and 3.

Finish off.

On **right** side rows, work Chart from **right** to **left**; on **wrong** side rows, work Chart from **left** to **right**.

Row
- 80
- 71
- 61
- 51
- 41
- 31
- 21
- 11
- 1

5. FLOCKS OF GEESE

Shown on page 11.

◼◼◼◻ INTERMEDIATE

Finished Size: 49¹/₂" x 61" (125.5 cm x 155 cm)

MATERIALS

Worsted Weight Yarn: **MEDIUM 4**

Pink - 34¹/₂ ounces, 1,875 yards
(980 grams, 1,714.5 meters)
Variegated - 12¹/₂ ounces, 710 yards
(360 grams, 649 meters)
Green - 12¹/₂ ounces, 680 yards
(360 grams, 622 meters)
Crochet hook, size H (5 mm) **or** size needed
for gauge
Bobbins or jaw hair clips

GAUGE: In pattern, 11 hdc = 4" (10 cm);
12 rows = 4¹/₄" (10.75 cm)

Work hdc in space **before** next hdc *(Fig. 4, page 3)* and in space **before** turning ch throughout.

Gauge Swatch: 4"w x 4¹/₄"h
(10 cm x 10.75 cm)
With Pink, ch 12.
Row 1: Hdc in second ch from hook and in each ch across: 11 hdc.
Rows 2-12: Ch 1, turn; hdc in first sp and in each sp across.
Finish off.

Wind each color onto bobbins *(see Bobbins, page 2)*. It is strongly recommended that you work the outlined square of the chart, page 19, as a process of familiarizing yourself with the color changes *(see Changing Colors, page 3)* and working with bobbins. This will also aid you in determining the yardage needed for each bobbin in the design.

COLOR KEY

☐ pink	♥ green	▲ variegated

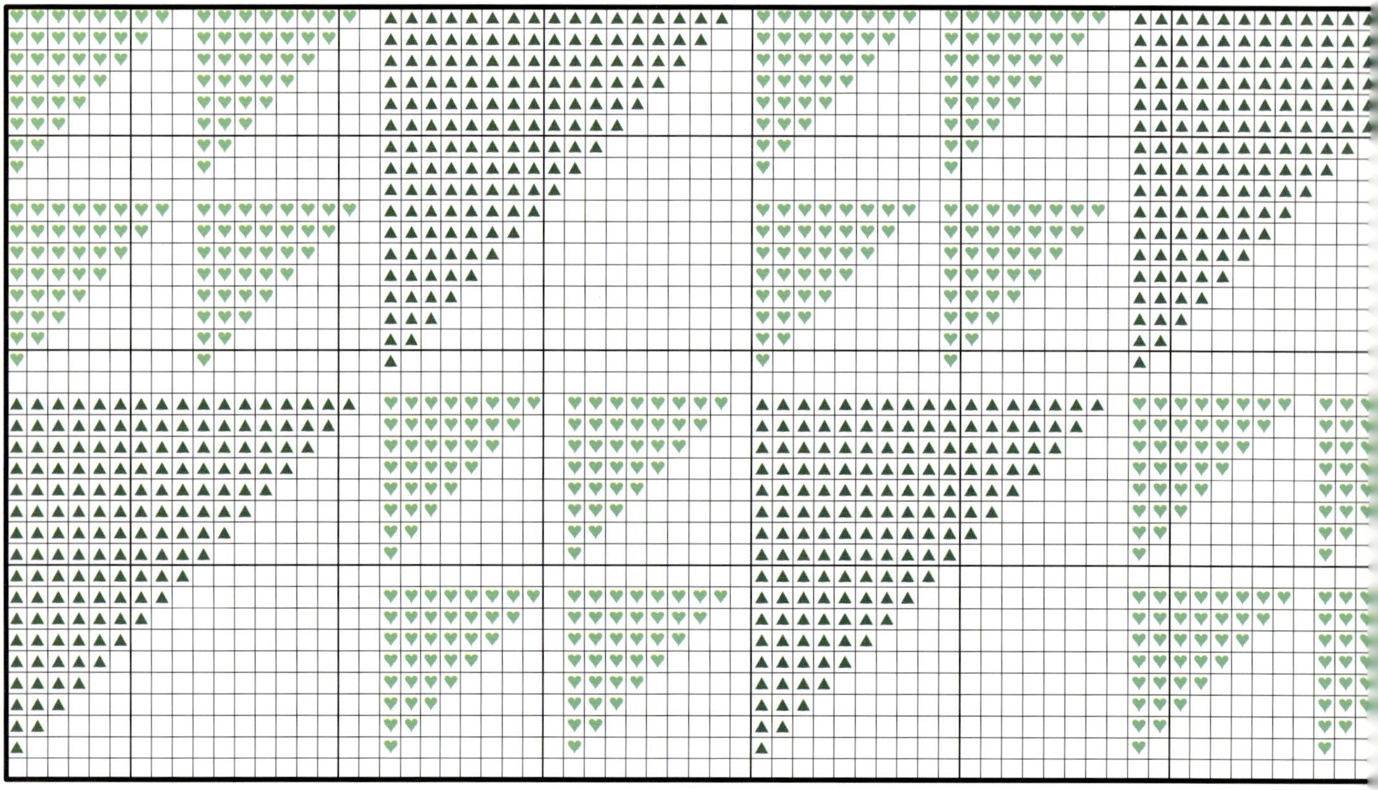

AFGHAN BODY

With Pink, ch 127.

Row 1 (Right side): Hdc in second ch from hook and in each ch across changing to Variegated in last hdc made: 126 hdc.

Note: Loop a short piece of yarn around any stitch to mark Row 1 as **right** side.

Work hdc in space **before** next hdc *(Fig. 4, page 3)* and in space **before** turning ch throughout.

Continue changing colors in same manner throughout.

Row 2: Ch 1, turn; hdc in first sp changing to Pink, ★ hdc in next 17 sps changing to Green, hdc in next sp changing to Pink, hdc in next 8 sps changing to Green, hdc in next sp changing to Pink, hdc in next 8 sps changing to Variegated, hdc in next sp changing to Pink; repeat from ★ 2 times **more**, hdc in last 17 sps.

Rows 3-36: Follow Chart below; at end of Row 36, change to Pink, cut Green and Variegated.

Rows 37-162: Follow Chart Rows 1-36, 3 times; then Rows 1-18 once **more**; at end of Row 162, change to Pink, cut Green and Variegated.

EDGING

Rnd 1: Ch 1, turn; 3 hdc in first sp, hdc in next sp and in each sp across to last sp, 3 hdc in last sp; working in end of rows, skip first row, hdc in next row and in each row across to last row, skip last row; working over beginning ch and in sps **before** hdc, 3 hdc in first sp, hdc in next sp and in each sp across to last sp, 3 hdc in last sp; working in end of rows, skip first row, hdc in next row and in each row across to last row, skip last row; join with slip st to first hdc: 580 hdc.

Continued on page 20.

On **right** side rows, work Chart from **right** to **left**; on **wrong** side rows, work Chart from **left** to **right**.

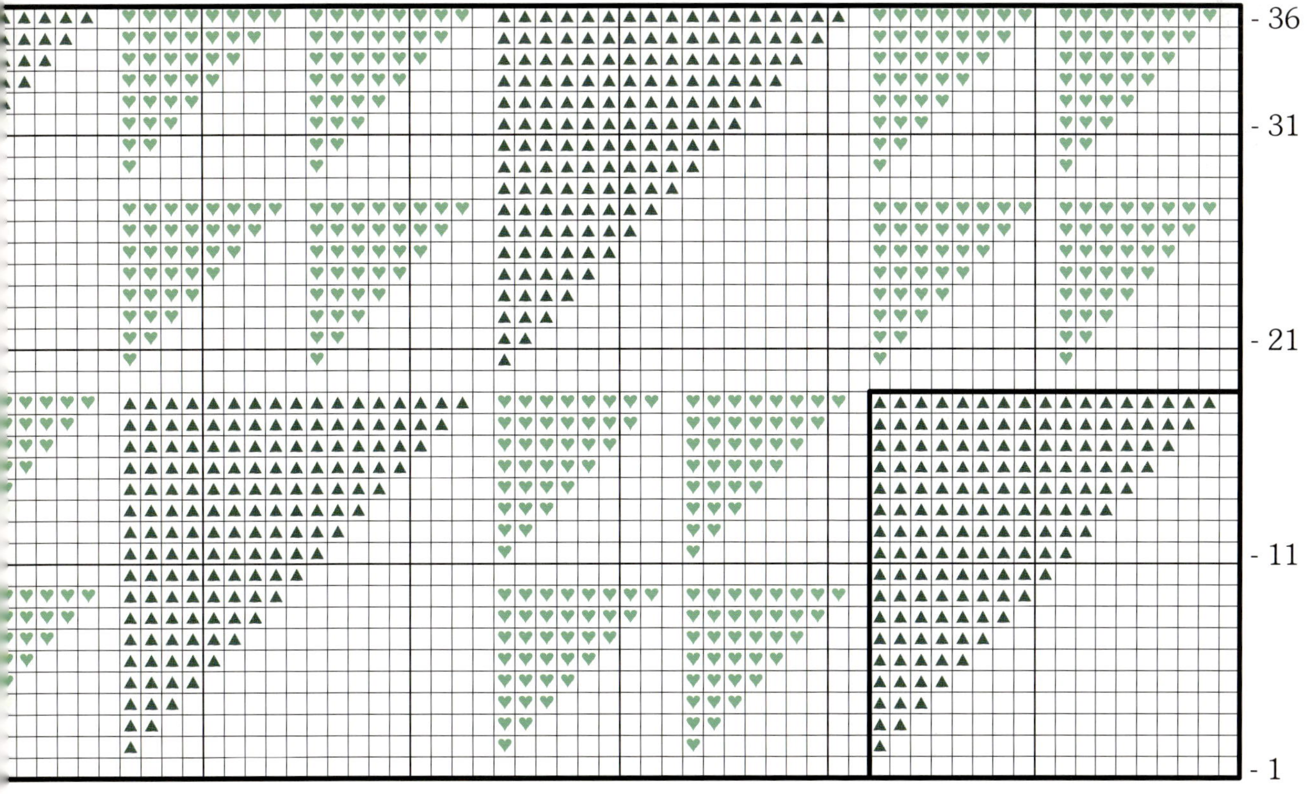

Rnd 2: (Slip st, ch 1, hdc) in first sp, 2 hdc in next sp, ★ hdc in next sp and in each sp across to next corner 3-hdc group, 2 hdc in each of next 2 sps; repeat from ★ 2 times **more**, hdc in next sp and in each sp across, hdc in same sp as first hdc; join with slip st to first hdc.

Rnd 3: (Slip st, ch 1, 3 hdc) in first sp, ★ hdc in next sp and in each sp across to second hdc of first 2-hdc group, 3 hdc in next sp; repeat from ★ 2 times **more**; hdc in next sp and in each sp across; join with slip st to first hdc.

Rnds 4 and 5: Repeat Rnds 2 and 3.

Finish off.

YARN INFORMATION

Each Afghan in this leaflet was made using worsted weight yarn. Any brand of worsted weight yarn may be used. Remember, to arrive at the finished size, it is the GAUGE/TENSION that is most important, not the brand of yarn.

For your convenience, listed below are the specific yarns used to create our photography models.

1. LOG CABIN
Patons® Décor
  Lt Blue - #1620 Pale Country Blue
  Green - #1611 Aqua
  Variegated - #1695 Mountain Top
  Blue - #1622 Rich Country Blue
  Purple - #1626 Aubergine

2. DOUBLE IRISH CHAIN
Bernat® So Soft®
  Tan - #70522 Dk Heather
  Black - #9876 Black
  Brown - #75029 Walnut Brown

3. PINWHEEL
Patons" Décor
  Yellow - #1659 Pale Bronze
  Lt Coral - #1650 Pale Coralberry
  Coral - #1651 Coralberry
  Lt Green - #1635 Pale Sage Green
  Green - #1636 Sage Green

4. WHIRLIGIG
Patons® Décor
  Yellow - #1659 Pale Bronze
  Blue - #1621 Country Blue

5. FLOCKS OF GEESE
Red Heart® TLC® Essentials™
  Pink - #2772 Lt Country Rose
  Variegated - #2966 Water Lily
  Green - #2672 Lt Thyme